PASSION MAPS

PASSION MAPS

✳

poems by

Adrianne Kalfopoulou

RED HEN PRESS | Los Angeles, California

PASSION MAPS

Library of Congress Cataloging-in-Publication Data

Kalfopoulou, Adrianne.
  Passion maps / Adrianne Kalfopoulou. — 1st ed.
    p. cm.
  ISBN 978-1-59709-158-9
  I. Title.
  PS3611.A4328P37 2009
  811'.6—dc22

                    2009027653

The Annenberg Foundation, the James Irvine Foundation,
and the National Endowment for the Arts partially support Red Hen Press.

Published by Red Hen Press
Los Angeles, CA
www.redhen.org
First Edition

for Korina, πάντα με αγάπη

Acknowledgements

My thanks to the editors of the following journals where these poems appeared, sometimes in different forms:

"Letters Home" *Prairie Schooner*; "Mute as Lawns Nobody Dares Walk Across" *Beloit Poetry Journal*; "Window", "Fall Grapes" *Poems & Plays #14*; "Balkan Voices" (as "Holy Agony") *Valparaiso Poetry Review* (www.valpo.edu/english/vpr); "The Border" *Crab Orchard Review* (issue on migration); "Cathedral" *Elixir*; "Random Heaven" *The Spoon River Poetry Review*; "Numbers in War", "Below the Cemetery", "Brides" *The Drunken Boat* (www.thedrunkenboat. com); "Cut Tomatoes", "I Marvel" *Pavement Saw*; "The Evening Drink" *Diner*; "Glass" *DMQ, Disquieting Muses Quarterly* (www.dmqreview.com); "Guerilla Lessons" *Atlanta Review* (issue on Greece); "He Wants Me to Describe It" (prize winner) *Room of One's Own*; "Opened" *Spire*; "The Meal" *Columbia Poetry Review*; anthologized in *Letters to the World, Poems from the Wom-Po Listserv*; "Setting Out" in *Ars Poetica* (http://www.logolalia.com/ arspoetica/archives/); "Those Times", "Her Sexy Hunger" *Attic*.

"Letters Home", "Her Sexy Hunger", "Brides", "Seams", "Fall Grapes" "Ritual" and *"Stassi Ecclesia"* appear in *CUMULUS*, a chapbook from Finishing Line Press.

Warm gratitude and thanks for my poetry friendships, με αγάπη to tryfon, ae, katerina, christopher, moira, nick, and joe and judy; a special thank you to joe powell for his patience with all my questions! And many φιλια to all you red hens.

Contents

VITAL CARTOGRAPHY

LAST SUPPERS

Stassi Ecclesia

Holy Agony

Passion Maps

Vital Cartography

"Those who set sail know that things will not be the same as at home. Explorers are prepared. But for us, who travel along the blood vessels, who come to the cities of the interior by chance, there is no preparation."
—*The Passion*, Jeanette Winterson

Guerrilla Lessons

1

The space is cold,
the bars are my mother's eyes.
A first winter
in a foreign land.
I am being told this is
our new life.
My mother promises
a bicycle,
my crying does not stop.
It is freezing. She sits
on the bed edge in blue light.
My father in underwear, is awake.
My tears
send him back to sleep.
Through my mother's night shift,
her body, fragile
and blue.

2

I am cold.
I am wearing a Caldor-bought
winter coat
at the dinner table.
I have never been in this country before,
America, Connecticut, freezing
in mid January.

3

In the middle of snow
the Doberman's head
got into the frame of the picture.
She barked and barked

and barked through that first winter,
so he bought a collar
that sent short shocks into
her throat, and the bark
faded to a whimper.
My mother decorated the rooms
in Persian carpets, rich
kilims, heavy curtains.
I learned her interior design.
Not that I wanted to pick at
flesh cross-sections,
but the intricate skeins
are tapestries.

4

The hunger,
like the fervent kisses of
every lover, is deep.
Every fulfillment, a possibility
of disaster: blasted soil,
scattered bird screams.
About to piss
my father was almost blown to bits
in the mountains. Death
is everywhere in the mountains—German mines
soldiers, military convoys.

I let myself fall in love
with the scalpeled light—almost jealous
he slapped me. Criminal,
this determination to steal
light, take its mouth
into my mouth,
resuscitate death.

5

When did I
become the enemy?
In an old schoolhouse
in a Greek mountain village
he shot a soldier in the face.
In *Carpenisi* (the story I remember),
he turned in the stairwell
to see the enemy, suddenly.

6

My father's lesson—
be stoic
in brutal combat.
Saltine crackers in a freezing swamp—
he enacts the battlefield
in the family. I am learning.
I am unable (like him
in the swamp) to leave.

7

Knees muddied,
nails ripped (beggar, refugee,
guerrilla fighter), I scrounge
for what I can dig up—
In the body's crevices,
the nectar, juice that feeds.
I am the survivor-thief—
When he looks
for the enemy
I cannot be
what is destroyed, the face
blown apart in the stairwell.

The plate of soup is pale with tears.
You will eat it he yells.

My mother's eyes are jailed,
her mouth sewn.
She makes life sounds.

8

One learns
to love
the bruised flesh
until it becomes the only body,
recurring.
Life is all drama
he murmured, haunted.
My waist curves deepened,
I became curious of their contours.

9

I will always move toward
the male figure;
his faces, colors, scents,
have never had anything in common
except for this ability
to return me
to the heart I am
now dissecting: the parts
I touch.

The Evening Drink

The wait for the boat brought us here
three hours too early to board
but then my father needs the whiskey,
the ritual of ordering ice, a bowl of nuts,
the drink, his nightly panacea, so the waves
and ink darkness might be sipped
at his ease, the talk kept muffled
against what he knows is the storm
beyond language breaking its madness
against the stern of his heart.

Numbers in War

A loaded gun, this silence of his,
each piece of story unloads
the quiet, this history
rotating death, forty-one shots
in the mountains, all of them for
Nazi Germans, except for
the woman, a German-Greek, a fact
he admits with the comment
that he wishes he had shot more,
more death, more of them
for all the slaughtered Greeks
in *Kolokythia*, a village
west of Lamia, uttered with the date
they executed 40 soldiers and 1 woman,
April 9, 1943 in *Kolokythia*,
hardly enough he adds,
keeping track of a Nazi command:
for every German dead, Hitler ruled
100 non-Germans would die,
and if not soldiers then civilians.
For every German wounded
the ratio dropped 50 to 1, fractions
my father tabulates as my daughter *shush*es
her cousin who asks her to pass
the pie, '*papou*' she interrupts,
'how many did you say
you killed?' as he goes silent
rotating his glass of wine, swirling
the red in circles.

"Are You Listening?"

We begin with practical things, the washing machine
that doesn't work, my unemployment benefits,
but before I know it I'm coughing tears
telling my mother after years
I can't seem to speak about what really scares me,
as she tells me my father worked all his life
in dangerous places 'for us' so we could have
what we have. Saigon. Phnom Penh. Jakarta.
Countries of emerald leaves, bread fruit trees,
fried bananas, the sticky rice I loved to eat.
'Dangerous places' she repeats
and I'm inside bullet marked walls, inside
the back bedroom where war was not meant to reach
where my brother is asleep—
the music box in his hands, the tiny ballerina
twisting stiffly in her one dance when we find him
on the stairs cradling her faint song,
my mother unable to explain the mysterious way
he sleepwalked, a soundless sampan floating
down a mined Mekong. 'Are you listening?'
I'm saying, 'You never listen to what I'm really saying.'
The flooded shame, urine soaked sheets,
scared as my father checked the streets.
The Vietcong outside, and inside
my mother irritated at having to change the bedding.
More urine soaked sheets. And the war went on
and we left Saigon and years later my mother tells me
not to make such a fuss about a stupid machine.

Seams

The pins like staples in rough silk
crinkled the fabric, pinching it in
so I could hardly wiggle, but did
and thought *breathe*; no,
don't breathe, if I could risk it,
the breadth of my self
barely held in. If I breathed out
the pins would turn in, needle
my sides, line themselves up against my skin,
prick and pin me further in.

Then I realized the dress
was not meant to fit. I needed to get it off
my limbs, slipped over my head
those pins would scratch my lids,
dance unchecked, poke
my neck. Pulled down
they snagged my thighs,
left threads of red, then over
my head again they stung my lips,
stabbed my chin, but
the falling metal tings,
the scattered clinks over marble,
the nicks gone from my skin,
the dress unraveled, left a nakedness
so sheer I couldn't bare it.

Setting Out

I set out, not for Byzantium, those lingering cartographies of bygone lives,
the lyric ruin of cities, the icons and burnt calligraphies of bygone lives.

I set out for New World opportunity, aerobic energy, fruit-flavored coffees,
perfected trilogies, imperfect in the piecemeal biographies of bygone lives.

I set out for those highways veering off byways, deer on patches of grass,
new News with a seductive prize, hard to imagine in the mysteries of bygone lives.

I set out for happiness, the flesh in love, couldn't get enough. Raw gifts in silk,
lipsticks, the one-way tickets, had me craving the bodies of bygone lives.

I set out for the city, lost my wallet, passport, VISA, any evidence of my name,
backtracked, discovered that I lacked tack, hard facts, the histories of bygone lives.

I set out without a map, just stories like this one, that Byzantium was holy,
the sages artful, drunk as the goldsmiths in love with the glories of bygone lives.

But here, far from any ancient place, here where we refuse to age and I buy products
for my face, I set out with my severed name, Calfo cut off from bygone lives.

American Vignettes

'What is America?' she said. 'A   hole in the water/'
—Tryfon Tolides, "Immigrant"

1

Grey expanse of Atlantic cloud,
the sudden edge of America. Perfectly roofed
houses, patches of yard. A country
in full summer, rich in poverty,
second hand cars, pension plans.
There is no one to meet me, only the stores
where I buy cosmetics, saleswomen
who smile as they would at anyone.
Dawn seeps in a new air conditioned day.

2

I need an address on checks,
my passport is not enough.
The name I have
is longer than it's supposed to be.
My father chopped it
afraid he would be sent back
to the old country where he could not
save money. Here the fat of the land
is in our Life's Savings,
all the fat we want, but no fruits
and few vegetables.

3

I am excited I can do things to my face,
inject a chemical, it's an idea
like the beauty of being here. The deer are stunned
by the highways. Distance is there to catch.
Cut roots. Go fast. Lift the lawns.

Houses are carried across the country
on the backs of trucks,
Greek village donkeys carry hay this way.
A friend tells me his parents set the temperature at 71
all year round on Long Island,
his childhood had no seasons.
Now he suffers from the heat in Greece,
wishes he could afford more shirts.

4

My brother-in-law's T-shirts burned
his Jersey house down, stacked so high
the fabric touched the closet ceiling bulb,
caught fire *like lit leaves*, my mother's eyes,
a motherland heartbreak, consumed.

5

Not too orange she murmurs, *bisque*.
The woman from Russia glides
foundation over my face.
She wants to lighten my eyes, I want her to stay
attentive, my mother couldn't,
she kept her gifts wrapped, sorrow-full.
3 panties for the price of 2.
Get 1 free, the cashier doesn't stop smiling,
everyone enjoys a toast,
the Atlantic crashes itself over the Jersey coast.

Looks & Wants

The issue of poverty is the issue of peace, there has been colossal instability created by poverty;
1/5 of the world lives on less than 1$ a day, and that's the growing part of the world.
—President of the World Bank (2003)

We want to remember from histories no longer ours, erect statues for museums,
build parks to look after; we want our closets full of clothes, 2s & 3s of everything
we can afford. We're sold on the deal. TV tells us we want the world safer: *we are*
planning for major humanitarian efforts . . . we did not expect to find such a
deteriorated infrastructure . . . we will not give money to governments who do not
want to help their people.

The conductor on Amtrak announces apologies when the lights go off, and again
when the heat goes off, apologies and thanks for our patience. He looks happy.
A girl points at snow-covered weeds in a swamp, says 'look at the corn, Mom!'

A lone goat wandering over abandoned air conditioning ducts looks lost. The mother
explains it's not corn though the weeds look pretty frozen. I keep looking for
the right sunglasses—oval-shaped by Ralph the saleswoman says look good. 'We're
just looking' I tell the GAP salesman who says, 'awesome.' 'Look out for the gap,'
the conductor warns as we get off the train.

In the Mall a woman and I wait in a glass enclosure looking for our rides.
She speaks with a Spanish accent, 'I try to start early to finish with the presents'.
She has fleshy hands I imagine cook good meals and give firm hugs. She tells me she
was looking at a WILLIAMS-SONOMA coffee machine, says 'it was so expensive.'
I suggest she look for better buys. She agrees but the coffee machine is the one
her son has been looking for.

The TACO BELL executive says the Chinese want a tangier Taco. He's pleased
TACO BELL has a competitive advantage over McDonald's. He wants
the China market to expand, 'We're in 12 out of 13 provinces. And next year we want
to be in Tibet.' The interviewer wants to know 'Is the product you're selling the same
as what you sell in the States?' 'It's basically the same' the executive answers,
'but the Chinese want to have more spice.'

We want to know why the NJ Transit didn't show up, the conductor on the Hoboken line looks confused, the looks of war-torn Samarra on the cover of today's newspapers make people look serious: *The bloodiest engagement since US troops occupied Iraq in April. The blizzard of gunfire devastated the city of Baghdad.*

'Is this the look of freedom? Is this what America wants?' chant the devastated. America wants to improve its economy; the woman at the ORIGINS counter wants to improve my looks. I want their products, especially their *Ginger Soufflé*. She wants me to try the neck firming cream.

Critical Maps

I must walk into this, I thought, carrying my tarnished wishes,
—Laurie Sheck, from *Black Series*

Map # 1 (found map)

Unlike Columbus
who looked outward, sure he found what he
was looking for, I find
an inner country
—blueberries,
someone who says
'Enjoy your stay', words like *preposterous*,
skin which bleeds, people I have nothing to do with,
pages and pages of photographs, faces
that look into futures
they believe will receive them.

Map #2 (lived map)

My love (though I never called him that)
spent half a year
taking our future apart, now
that map is piecemeal.
Like children we mistake the lit heart
for a plaything and go map-less
until we blister,
burn our palms,
until we learn
to properly cook
our meals.

Map # 3 (school map)

Knowledge
can set fires (could Einstein know his map for peace
would inflame cities).

Map #4 (homemade map)

Love is rabid,
unable to understand
why it bites.

Map #5 (discovered map)

Love, true love,
has little to do with the above.
Love, as they say, is blind,
part darkness, part willingness.
The Sufi poet,
Omar Khayyam (c. 1047- c. 1122),
was given a book
by a judge of the high court
to write his verses in.
In Shamara Kande (now Afghanistan)
Omar Khayyam was tried
for reciting love poetry
instead of verses
from the Koran;
the judge's brother
executed for the same insurrection,
became an example.
Before the high court, the judge
made a present of a book of

blank pages to Khayyam
with the advice to
write his poems,
believing it unwise to risk one's life for
personal loves.

Map #6 (historical map)

Shamara Kande, a small village,
was burned to the ground
by Mongol invaders,
but Omar Khayyam's book survived
(translated by Edward Fitzgerald
in the 19th century). Khayyam
went into tradition because he, like
Columbus, went against it
unknowingly,
Columbus believing
he had found India as he sailed
counterclockwise (to avoid
Ottoman ships—the known world)
and backwards,
discovered America, Khayyam
because he wrote of a love
he preferred to sing.

Map #7 (invented map)

Cartographers
beginning with Claudius Ptolemaeus
in the second century
mapped according to
what they found

as opposed to what they believed.
I found words preposterous—
'I could be with you
for life' amounted to five months,
his words useless
liras, drachmas, pesetas,
souvenirs for tourists; the euro
like *efficiency,* like *greed,*
now common currency.

Map #8 (misread map)

The lust for conquest
changed maps.
Appalled by our thirst,
we pretend
it is right to forget
how we made love.
Abandonment is its own map,
the Native-Americans on reservations.
The Native-Americans
took freedom entirely
for granted.

Yassir

*In the spring of 1920, Mustafa Kemal ordered the people of my mother's village in
the Pontic Mountains to be sent on a death march to exile into the Syrian desert.*
—Thea Halo, *Not Even My Name*

There are names, *Aybasti,*
Niksar, Iondone, once villages
where chamomile and blood poppies grow
where the stones, quiet
as those who may know, belonged
to whole towns
now erased by the grass.
Then a boy, the Turk in his eighties
remembers helping his neighbors
spread manure, talks of
how it nurtured the crops.
The families were blacksmiths, weavers,
farmers who gathered in the village square,
not in preparation for the August festival
or to dance the *kotsari* to the *kementze.*
This time Turks who tolled the church bells,
ordered those gathered to walk,
not to stop walking, away
from what they knew of home; they carried
newborns, the not-yet-born, small cloth pockets
of grain, sometimes gold coins as the freshly
churned fields, familiar skies, became
death fields and skies.

I was grateful for the cowhide moccasins
grandfather had made for me
Themia thinks; she is ten, one of hundreds,
then one of the thousands that
became the hundreds of thousands

ordered by Kemalist soldiers
to keep walking, the pots and pans
buried on the land, a favorite calf left
tethered to an apple tree,
the fireplace *where grandfather told tales*
and played the viol like the ravines and pear trees,
the color of bread, people scattering seed
for another harvest, lost
as the walk grew long, as *each day soldiers*
on horseback were replaced
with other soldiers, as the trees
grew smaller, the rocks taller, as sand
blew into parched mouths, feet burned
over the baking earth, and the world emptied
its hills and scents and the soldiers
continued to whip those who could still walk
clutching dead babies the soldiers
would not allow buried,
forcing the dead to be left
on roadsides, lying on stone walls,
though sometimes
someone dug a quick grave with his hands,
as they continued to walk into the sky's infinity
murmuring a language almost gone.

Letters Home

*In 1846 Margaret Fuller settled in Italy sending articles to the New York
Daily Tribute of Giuseppe Mazzini's effort to establish a Roman Republic.
She also fell in love and gave birth. In 1850 she, Ossoli, and their two-year old
son, drowned in a shipwreck off of Fire Island on their way back to America.*

I try to imagine Rieti, you pregnant, the small room
scent of sun and dampness, then

a Rome under siege, *Mio caro, Mio amore*
you write Ossoli from Rieti, *My husband is Roman*, in a letter

to your mother, *of a noble but now impoverished house.
In him I have found a home*, in him is *a great*

native refinement. In Rieti, daily to Ossoli, words of
anxiety . . . so ignorant with a baby

these first days of his life. Then from Florence, *our little boy
grows better in the air*. After leaving America

you come upon sorrow's terraced hills,
the body of ardor. *My strength has been taxed to the utmost*

*to live. I have been deeply humiliated finding myself
inferior to many noble occasions, but precious*

lessons have been given you write Emerson, who does not
understand why you stay on amid *bread and grapes . . . and pain.*

You explain *I want human beings to love. I have much
to do and learn in Europe. Methinks I have my part therein,*

and begin to speak Italian, eat *figs, the most delicious . . .
for five or six cents*. Your newborn near death,

then cholera as close as Bologna, *we think we have money
to last till April*, in Tuscany *the purple grape hangs garlanded*

from tree to tree. But there was never time *to know the sum total—
to reflect.* Fires burned in Rome *O Rome, my country*

you confess, and describe Mazzini, *the inspiring soul
of his people* who could not save Rome

as the Romans *fought like lions, betrayed by France.*
You leave Angelino with a wet nurse.

*I saw blood stream on the wall where Ossoli was.
I have a piece of bomb that burst close to him,* the gunshot

wounded take up the days. There is *always rain,*
the too cold rooms, *the suffering men, solace in tending*

to the suffering men as you write Emerson again *I know not,
dear friend, whether I ever shall get home across that great ocean.*

In Italy, *feeding on ashes,* it becomes *useless to try and write
of these things, volumes would hardly begin to tell my thoughts,*

there are words of *the Mater Dolorosa, the fair young men
bleeding to death,* history outdoing your deepest loves.

Our destiny is sad; we much (sic) *brave it as we can.*

The Uneasy Equation of Space and Form

Συν+ χωρω *(with + space)* = Συγχωρώ *(forgiveness)*

　　　　1
I keep looking for Milosz' *more spacious form,* an open accordion of desire, a lung
expanding closing sheaves.

We travel to find space, lose it when we get lost. A coffee shop owner gives me
directions, form opens up, becomes

larger still when I thank him and he smiles, the sheaves far apart, lungs full of breath.
An email from a poet I've never met crosses over

in cyberspace. We speak across the divide, unlike the man whose love I thought
would cross continents, and didn't (form

collapsed). Fear coiled in on itself, circling air, shrinking form-less remains, two
emptied snake skins. Without him

space opens, though he waits for my messages (uncoiling); I keep them for myself,
resist predictable forms (his answers, which may or may not

come, taking up space). I am drawn to open forms, the mixed patterns on the young
woman at Penn Station in NYC in a tight ¾ checked jacket, jeans

w/ a velvet maroon stripe, a pink scarf, imagination exudes from her as it does
from beautifully formed artifacts, unlike the conservative chic

of 'the little black dress', I like unpredictable combinations of scarves and gloves,
synthetic leopard spots. The young woman in NYC stands out, formal

black evening wear blends in. Choice provides more form to choose from.
In Poland women combined colors in unusual ways, defying the circumstance

of lack, a barwoman wore a thick wool mini-skirt informally, her patent leather
boots probably her only pair. In NYC someone might have

looked like her, though more able to change forms (bargain sales). It's no accident
cruise ships have so many older people on them, as they travel

to the Easter islands, Brazil, shortened days expand into countries. 'You must know
we want to be there,' my father's voice long-distance

from a cruise ship the afternoon his mother died in an Athens hospital.
There was too much space to cross to be by her side.

I lay my cheek against her chilled skin, the clammy arms, kept kissing her stiff hands
until the nurse told me they had to take her form away.

I cried as the darkening hours closed into space without her. For months
space opened, formless. I faced it like an astronaut whose tie to her ship snaps

> without formal rules
> formed
> of formidable loss

2

Space becomes a sudden patience, the dishes washed, clothes put away, a letter from an
admirer; a privilege of faith. Did St. Francis of Assisi feel spacious as he laid his form in
a field overrun by mice as he endured their bites? Every time someone leaves me, space
opens, terrifying, then I touch myself unexpectedly. Words form the
absence

in which my grandmother repeated obsessively that she'd been good all her life, biting
down on gentleness like it was food, gambling kindness so she might form herself—
someone she liked—in others' eyes. Otherwise people cruise the seas, gather trinkets to
prove they've gone far enough to outrun forms they find themselves trapped
in

like regretful lovers, the way he thought we would be greedy for space though
we slept on a single bed without feeling crushed. Space grew in the shape of possibility,
until our appetites ate up possibility. My tears he said, close on him like a curtain
but he can't stop my crying as we are buried in a formless pain I cannot not
form

when my daughter comes home after the weekend with her father with talk of a
school friend who insulted a Lebanese girl without meaning to, then apologized
(sudden space). Another accused a friend of wearing false boobs the girl insisted were
hers (forced space), now the girl won't talk to her friend, though after an apology she
forgives

Xeni, Xeno, Xenitia

I wanted a history/to touch me and stay,
    —Nicholas Samaras, "In a Time of Fire"

Xeni I am called when I don't understand
the Greek a public servant insists
I must write in. My father learned
German in high school,
the language of the enemy
when the mountains of northern Greece
were full of *xena* troops
who butchered and were butchered.

My father is disoriented
by my coming to live in the country he was
exiled from after war, a place
displaced, while his
Greek self was replaced
in *xenitia*, a state of continuous
estrangement,
not without its blessings.

Para-xeni (more of
strange) to my father,
who generally considers women
complicated, I find it difficult to explain
the hospitality of this strangeness,
xeni to the ancients,
who understood the foreigner as *xenos*
both guest and stranger.

On the generous divide of otherness
unfamiliar to the self,
(the grounds, Anne Carson notes,

for ecstasy) coming into
one's own through (an)other
makes me think of
Margaret Fuller
in the village of Reiti
where she gave birth in anonymity.

It was Giuseppe Mazzini's dream to make Italy
a Republic, not prey to the other—
in his time, the Venetians.
Finally, a nightgown of skin,
the lees of her mind spume-soaked,
Fuller drowned
with her baby
and Ossoli
on *The Elizabeth*
wrecked off the coast of New England.
Her Italian sojourn
had made her *xeni*
to her own compatriots,
Hawthorne for example
who based Hester Prynne on Fuller's
having given birth out of wedlock.

For Hawthorne sensuous women
remained other,
and ecstasy, the ancients' notion
of union,
suspect.
Xeno to the Puritans
who took over a land never theirs,
the Native American continent remained

Satan's wilderness,
never a possibility
for ecstasy—which meant
one could not feel joy
in foreign lands, including
the self displaced, or
replaced by its own estrangement,
a fateful *xenitia*
I have fallen in love with.

Mute as Lawns Nobody Dares Walk Across

When my mother calls telling me of still freezing nights across the Atlantic,
I smell moldering pears, the claret tinge of their bruised skins, as mother talks of
her darkness, the not-good-news that travels from where she lives in thinner light,
her voice in low cadences as she speaks of Kiveli who made pies all her life, and

I smell moldering pears, the claret tinge of their bruised skins, as mother talks of
that awful man who rubbed Kiveli's face into the pavement and broke her elbow.
Her voice in low cadences as she speaks of Kiveli who made pies all her life and
lay bleeding on an Athens street when a young woman found her and asked if

that awful man who rubbed Kiveli's face into the pavement and broke her elbow
was someone she would recognize. *What man? What man?* Kiveli was crying and
lay bleeding on an Athens street when a young woman found her and asked if
with her face to the pavement she remembered the event. Remembered if the man

was someone she would recognize. *What man? What man?* Kiveli was crying and
asked over the phone if I wanted a bottle of oil from her olives, *For your salads?*
With her face to the pavement she remembered the event. Remembered if the man
had hurt her anymore she would not have been able to walk, but won't say more, and

asked over the phone if I wanted a bottle of oil from her olives, *For your salads?*
I tell my mother I'm going to see Kiveli, and mother tells me if her arthritic knee
hurts her any more she won't be able to walk, but won't say more, and
I ask about her surgery, whether her knee is healing, and say she'll be okay.

I tell my mother I'm going to see Kiveli, and mother tells me if her arthritic knee
gets any worse she will be left to the sad fact of a wheelchair life, so
I ask about her surgery, whether her knee is healing, and say she'll be okay.
Do you have memories that won't heal? the Vietnam vet asks, confessing had things

got any worse he would have been left to the sad fact of a wheelchair life, so
What man? What man? the therapist wants to know, *muffled voices, Vietnam.*
Do you have memories that won't heal? the Vietnam vet asks, confessing had things . . .
There was a coup d'état. I learned to count in Thai then we moved to Bangkok.

What man? What man? the therapist wants to know, *muffled voices, Vietnam.*
I had an uncle who thought it fun to slip my panties down in a circle of adults.
There was a coup d'état. I learned to count in Thai then we moved to Bangkok.
My uncle would say we played a game, the circle of adults nodded and laughed.

I had an uncle who thought it fun to slip my panties down in a circle of adults.
He died in a hospice speaking in Greek his American wife couldn't understand.
My uncle would say we played a game, the circle of adults nodded and laughed.
Kiveli is healing fine, back to making pies. We talk and I tell her of my uncle.

He died in a hospice speaking in Greek his American wife couldn't understand.
My mother says how sad to die speaking words your wife can't understand.
Kiveli is healing fine, back to making pies. We talk and I tell her of my uncle.
I'll revisit Vietnam, even Bangkok, *It all comes back,* the therapist insists.

My mother says how sad to die speaking words your wife can't understand.
And poor Kiveli, accosted by that man . . . What man? What man? . . .
I'll revisit Vietnam, even Bangkok, *It all comes back*, the therapist insists.
So I tell my mother about my uncle and she is uncomfortable, interrupts with

And poor Kiveli, accosted by that man . . . What man? What man? . . .
her darkness the not-good-news that travels from where she lives in thinner light,
her days mute as lawns nobody dares walk across, and I'm folding sweaters and scarves
when my mother calls, telling me of still freezing nights across the Atlantic.

My Father's Siestas

While now the noon light dims,
its hard relentless stare was never
fully in your face. What you spent life
making sure to curtain off,
and discipline, could not be tamed.
The August waves of heat, your children,
restless in those molten afternoons you slept,
were traitors to that routine.
Not allowed to speak, we counted every time
the bed sighed, muffled giggles
when someone pinched or tickled,
and learned in those long
childhood afternoons, it was dangerous
to thieve the stupor of dead sleep.

Mother Tongue

I always felt she would have preferred to sing
her words the way she stood in choir, part of the curve
of women in their choral robes who gave themselves
to song. Instead she swallowed arias, whole operas,
ignored what seethed, entire sentences of crooked turns
she chained to contain how she might feel
letting loose a ballad or hymn instead of watching
Frank Sinatra on television, keeping time to my father's
banal rhymes. It was 'let's have some wine'
when things were fine or 'you always whine' and she,
predictably, replied with her *I don't mind* and *that's fine*.

It was the pact she kept but didn't express, the way
she placed plain verbs like *see* and *eat* and *sleep*, faraway
from the dangers of *dare* and *rage* or *age* (when she
hardly breathed seeing him beat the anger out of me)
that taught the importance of listening to what was not said.
What I couldn't understand, like the sermons in church
by the priests speaking in Latin or Greek, I came to admire
for tone and somber murmurings, and the rapture
of everything the words didn't capture.

Neos Kosmos

a neighborhood in Athens

Garbage bins, low rent basement flats and immigrant workers coming home
in T-shirts, shorts and dust, carrying plastic bags of quick dinners,

exhausted hours in the hard-working last chink of light in this neighborhood where
there's hardly any. Discarded furniture's piled high next to trash,

shattered bricks of a building going up in a too-narrow lot where some young
family will move in with savings and a down payment on possibilities.

Debris crunches under the wheels. I park and think of my father, his home
in Athens taken by Nazi officers, then America's plush interiors

that never managed to keep out what stayed in—*I am most proud of that time
in the mountains. I was 16. There was no food in Athens. The German officers*

kept whatever there was for themselves he repeated in rooms where he promised
books, a chance to eat at the table of plenty though I could not eat what

he insisted I eat, as he tried to forget the dead by keeping us overfed.
I lock and leave the car, hear laughter from an open window, and someone's

lovemaking like deep breathing.

LAST SUPPERS

"Between the lover and the beloved," she replied, "there is no distance. There are words only through the power of desire, description through Taste."

—Rabi'a al-Adawiyya (717?-801)
Muslim woman mystic of Basra

Nurture

From S. Nicola, a small town of Caulonia in Calabria, my Grandpa Anthony left at 15 to arrive in Pittsburg PA where my Grandma Lena, his wife to be at 14, left her aunt's where she was being brought up, and married him in true love as she tells me at 97, though Grandpa Anthony died in his early 50s of night shifts in steel mills. In those days no one paid attention to what the workers breathed in and what he breathed out my Grandma Lena folded into her Christmas rolls, a recipe she kept secret until she gave it to me. I'd like my words to be as satisfying as Grandma's dough as I try to feed them to my lover as he tells me he destroys everything and I keep saying it's up to him not to. Simple as that, the way Grandpa Anthony left S. Nicola in Caulonia, a poor village, and made his way to an unknown America, a life with my grandmother now stooped with arthritis who still loves to make the nut rolls she rolls out on her own. The man who is my lover tells me he feels oppressed by what I say. And I tell him I come from people who struggled to transform what threatened them, Grandma Lena Demase (*Dimase* in Italian) made her rolls into her 90s, her fingers curved into commas, to feed us the sweet bread and took care of her mentally-challenged daughter my Aunt Marie who collected stamps until she died at home, happily, older than her father, Grandpa Anthony who left S. Nicola without any language except his native Italian, who learned English, badly, to express what it felt like to leave everything so he could arrive somewhere new.

Her Sexy Hunger

I remember the way *yiayia* loved
the pomegranates, how she reminded me
not to forget to get kilos of them in October,
their season, when the mottled yellows
were splashed in lucid pinks,
the reds a burgundy so rich you felt them
deepen into velvet. Still hanging
from their cut twigs, sometimes cracked,
those fruits showed their jeweled seeds
like an opening you can't resist.
She ate them that way too, her aged fingers
deft as her nails cut into the pulpy flesh, the layer of
clustered seeds that clung to the insides, fuchsia
pearls she brought to her lips and sucked
with so much satisfaction.

Stupid Fights

... I'd rather just go to the beach
    —Rebecca Byrkit

When it surges in me, a lava heat, the anger makes its own demands.

Calm, I can't imagine what gets me to send a wallet, cell phone ...
flying across the table to scatter wherever it all lands.

Holding onto my scarf while clutching someone speeding on a motorbike
I know I have to grab tight or I'll be blown away

trying to catch a stupid scarf. I could topple off, my skull crack on asphalt
like Humpty Dumpty's. I guess (or that's what I'm trying to explain) you hardly

realize you're about to risk your life for something idiotic—a flying hat or scarf
or the livid storm his words can stir, this everyday stuff: you know

the real reasons—tragedy, the stolen happiness of the undeserving,
paralyses you like car beams in an animal's eyes, the rest of it,

making sure you have ingredients for the Mexican dinner, snapping off dead
geranium blooms, screaming at him, is meant to make you feel better.

The Meal

You give me caviar on crackers,
I make you ginger chicken.
You bring me special chocolates,
I tell you of artichokes cooked in lemon.
You show me garlic melts in stir-fried broccoli,
I show you how to boil basmati.
You find a rare merlot for Christmas,
I choose thick salmon slabs for dinner.
You speak of Guatemala coffee,
I offer 'Tahini with some honey?'

You learn my tastes, I spiral
fingers down your face. Teach me
how to pace my kisses
as we do this sifting of the right amounts
for mixing the spice of how
you touch my secret spine, salt the movement
we get caught in—a thing not always fed—
this coming back for more
is now my climb along your shore,
baste these knees and thighs in gourmet sweat,
lick the curves and crevices
of all that's on your plate,
swallow joy like champagne.

He Wants Me to Describe It

My friend wants to know what I think of
when I panic. I pause in front of lit shop windows of long
wrap-around scarves, beaded necklines and Indian silks.
Absence, abandonment are the words
but they don't satisfy him. Our kids are in a bakery
calling us to taste how quickly meringue
melts on the tongue, how sweet it is. We forget it's late
until we say goodbye.

He will go back to his apartment with his daughter
who will soon go back to her mother in New York.
I will drive home on the night road
where I almost met oblivion. His daughter will cry
because she doesn't want to leave, my daughter will cry
because she doesn't know why Christmas didn't feel like Christmas.
I will remember how easily the car wheels skidded
off the wet road in a new year rain.

When I panic I think of that wide desert space,
the expanding field of it, the harsh, cold swallow of hope
in a black night drive when the roads are wet and you have had
too much to drink and desperately want to reach home, the feeling
is as still as a punished child waiting to slam its fist into the door.

(A)stray

The one confesses he is a famished baby, the other welcomes the greedy
child; for an instant they merge within the hospitality ritual.

—Julia Kristeva, "Toccata and Fugue for the Foreigner"

He speaks
of keeping in touch
as if folding
a napkin from his lap,
the good meal over,
the company now ready for sleep.
In the rock shadow
of an island afternoon
words explained
how hard the distance
to recovery, how impossible
circumstance becomes (there's the kids,
even a wife upstairs,
not mad, not
locked in any attic).
So the fateful meeting
in city drizzle,
the breathless confession
and possession,
the banquet eaten
in good stead,
is poisoned. Let bitterness
blister, let fate, cold life,
the heedless twists of heart feelings
stir a witch-poison.

Wrap the widow in black,
blanche her lips, prepare her
lifelong dismay.

Isn't that the book story?
the fairytale gone astray.
The children want
to urge the nightmare away.
We tell them
it's a bad dream,
remember Sleeping Beauty
is kissed
by a Prince, Red Riding Hood
climbs out alive
from inside the wolf.
Who is it? they insist.
What's that dark shadow?
Peter Pan flying to Tinker Bell?
The book of tales
we enter so wholly
to recognize love
warns the unrescued
are clearly damned.
Who was he?
Count Dracula? Beautiful in his hunger
for the sweet kiss
he so perfectly consumed.

Fall Grapes

We didn't know the acrid scent of trodden grapes
stewing in their ferment. We mistook the flushed skins

for sweet juices, bit the thick-fleshed fruit,
learned these clusters were meant for the barrels,

ready to be mashed: pulp and stems, seeds, stray leaves
churned to sift the liquid out of bitterness, what we did

in love without admitting the skin we licked
along each other's necks was *mustos*, the taste of

what our bodies could not change, what others turn into wine.

I Marvel

at how I smile, make coffee
in the morning, spread the wet grounds, smell
the black liquid drip, enjoy the heat as I sit
in the quietly breaking day.
I marvel that I am able to think of
a month from now, plan a vacation, realize
the day will have me teach, drive to school
and back, pause at a fruit stand, hold
the pomegranate's shape, the garlic's curved
clove nape. I'm amazed I wash
the soap from my face, dry my skin, feel
its tightness with delight, see everything
transformed into beloved light as though I've found
my best friend's hand in blind night.

At the Edge of the World

We reached the cluster of blue tables,
rickety, straw-backed chairs
badly painted. Goats
edged close. You talked to them.
We sat. The long walk
over the hill, made us hungry.
The mountain slope
looked charcoaled,
the moon's sliver
was just visible.
Waves caressed loose rocks,
the goats moved into the hillside.
Bare light bulbs
swung above the tables,
a surly waiter made a jibe
about our refusal to order beets
from a tin. It didn't matter
that the food was late,
the feta mediocre, we still talked of
never leaving, of
not having any idea how
we would outlive
the peace of that evening.
Fired color poured into the sea,
the mountains became prehistoric beasts.
We drank more ouzo.
I acted like we had time
for more walks.
The sun gradually sank its red,
the children ran
to see a last lighted pin tip
behind the lowest mountain ridge.
You said this was

one of the happiest moments
of your life. Bread crusts
and onion slices
swam in olive oil, napkins stayed
wadded under our plates.
The brine was thick
with seaweed, the moon's silver
widened over the sea.
Against the tide, moored boats
clapped their hulls, and the Milky Way
spilled stars.

Window

I fly there. To that bed next to that window onto the trees, in that bed
where you first saved me from nightmares I ground with my teeth.
Did you kiss my cheek or caress it in my sleep?

Outside the window sparrows flew, clustering in the high branches.
Asleep inside, I dreamt skies and rivers, restless greens, like birds
we couldn't believe the sudden sky above those trees.

What rogue happiness, that summer breeze, the light's generous portions,
the shadows sheathed, playful over the tousled sheets where
we didn't expect to be. Outside we watched the satiated families,
lovers kindled in their warmth. Chilled,
we touched; the glass disappeared, summer's green heat in that room,
its resin scents—the birds, confused, reckless in their flight

high above the balconies and streets, flew straight into the clear pane—
the trees and sky so much clearer than what they couldn't see—and smashed their wings.

Cut Tomatoes

After Alexei Kyrilloff

Red
on a black canvas
background.
My life, seeded
in this
opened violence
of the vegetable
in halves
bleeding
color
through black.

Feminist Theory

She says I give her scraps for meals, nothing like
the mashed potatoes and pork chops
we have at a neighbor's, then the conversation
boils over in the car as she tells me she wonders
why I'm not gay because of the way I talk about men.
I answer evenly, but not for long since I'm livid about what
she calls scraps, lentils cooked between chores, the way
I forget I don't have celery and rush to the corner store.
The tomatoes from the organic place, better
than anything that go for tomatoes in the supermarket.
I even make sure she has the grapes she likes,
also from the organic shop, which means they're expensive.
And about men, I say, I guess I haven't had the luck.
She's mad I picked her up from her friend's,
or maybe it's because I'm taking her with me to dinner
at a friend of mine's, but she won't let up, 'you *always*
take the side of women! *Always*! And mom, you really get *illogical*.'
So I say, feeling this is much tougher than I expected,
'logic is the excuse a lot of men use for being cold-blooded
about things that are illogical to begin with . . .' I go on,
still hurt. 'And then they think they've given you the world
when they decide to give you anything.' She is quiet,
then says 'women act that way too, mom. You think you've
given everything and get upset when I say you haven't.'

The Body of This Car

When the whole mechanism for opening the door comes apart,
I know it's a matter of time. It has taken me so far, this
now faded machine with its sun-bleached roof cracking paint veins,
the ground eaten tires almost bald of tread from the travel.
I remember it new, the olive green shine of the beautiful metal,
its slick feel and even softer sheen, the way it sped through
so many streets, tricky and stubborn, nicked, hit, finally dented
in that one place that no longer made sense to fix,
the right door caves in when the sun spills over the length of it
so the accident scars show merciless surfaces. I'm murmuring
it has to make it through another two, three months, after all these years,
some fifteen, maybe more. I've stopped counting, I'm just hoping
the silicon-pumped tire doesn't burst as I watch another young mechanic
swipe his hands into the flapping interior, wring out the foam
I'd injected to keep the wheel going, knowing it was all a matter of time,
the final flat bang of the rubber that's already sliding too smoothly
on those curves, the last of my hub caps spinning off one night
as I drove home, surprised to see the shiny disc shoot across the street
like a meteorite, me going too fast to stop, so now the knobs look
the hard-knocked bolts they are, the steering wheel shorn too,
shredding its too-used surface, those hours of days of years of
my hands steering now peeling, but none of that bothers me,
not the way the street grit hits the chipped enamel or gathers in
the wheels' exposed crevices, or the sagging seat I have to pile pillows
onto so my back doesn't slip or the inside latch coming off the back door,
or the handful of dropped wires I wrap with black tape and shove back
in a space under the dashboard, none of it bothers me until I am explaining
to the mechanic who is eyeing the car like a surgeon, that I need it
a little longer. He tells me the car's silicone-pumped tire will hold out,
but not for long, then he's checking the dropped wires under the dashboard
to see if there's any connection with a flickering light, if maybe
the no-longer automatic windows I now wind up and down manually
might be part of an electrical glitch. I am suddenly self-conscious,
explaining how old the car is, how I've managed to keep it going,
he is not saying much, concentrating, his grease-stained hands busy.

The Benediction

Here the gifts have ribbons,
gossamer fringes and strips of glitter
under the decorated tree,
taller than the one my daughter trimmed,
and then beneath the spare branches,
she placed the small envelope of *koliva*
given in Ari's memory,
her young school friend killed
in a car accident 9 days before his 16th birthday.
She couldn't eat the handful of boiled wheat,
raisins and candied almonds meant to feed us
with his memory, so she left it there
and wants a moment of silence
before we unwrap the presents, asking
that we think of Ari and his family
even though this is America, and our small tree
with the packet of *koliva* beneath it
is in Greece where we will soon return,
while here, all the way in America,
we try to feel gratitude for this fortune.

Last Rites

Your skin thinned as rubbed fabric,
the sheen of fingertips holding the biscuit
I'm urging you to bite, as you
gradually chew, nodding on that bed,
your body hardly able, but still obedient
as I pull the sheet to your chin,
brush off crumbs, listen to you telling me
it was your bad luck to slip as your hip
smashed its bone to the tile, your whole life
thrown from under you as your leg
hit the floor, bounced from its socket, detached,
and I want to give you more of the biscuit, help you
savor the sweet you lick from your lips when
you ask me to draw the curtain against the light.

Ground

I think of the ripe olive, pulp on the tongue, the tomato's swimming seeds red
as young wine swallowed like communion blood and the body that lusts and the tastes
which name. People were bent over the spring hills today. From a distance I couldn't
tell what they were, leaning into wind like battered trees. The sky was radiant grey.
Further away were steel cranes. Then the broken road, a mud spill of water from an
open pipe I could call a vein and the rush of water, a force that spat back muck, what
won't or can't repair itself, not the blue trees and people pulling up roots to eat, but
the ripped earth seething, swallowing that.

Stassi Ecclesia

Stassi (Στάση): Greek for position as in to position oneself against, or to take a position; also colloquial for a stopping place such as a bus stop.

Eccelesia (Εκκλησία): From the ancient Greek meaning a general assembly or municipal gathering of citizens; the apostle Paul used the term to found the Pauline church or 'εκκλησία' and bring people together united in their worship of God.

Below the Cemetery

This is the road of the dead, shops
sell laminated photographs, faces
in garish colors sealed into marble headstones
as if permanence might be given
to what is gone, the edifices meant to
decorate absence. Winged angels, suppliant
and patient, robed Christs, even the odd cupid
line shelves of dust-filmed windows.
They don't commemorate the devils
like Giotto's frescoes. Passive as the shopkeepers
with their days-old beards, cigarettes,
their shirt collars vaguely soiled.
There is nothing here of ecstasy
or battle, not even the devastation of loss
unless this is finally what it looks like,
the men hardly aware of where they're standing,
in entranceways that display caskets,
frigid Madonnas, plastic flowers and tinny candelabra,
a welcome to an underworld that is daylight
thrown on what cannot be resurrected.

Cathedral

I understand
this given clarity, the pews
never filled,
how emptiness
echoes
through the eaves.
Love, your body
was my sacrament.
I'd known such completion
only in abstinence.
So I watched
for flaws,
stumblings,
to help me
forget you.
Nights had no shawl,
the darkness frightened me.
I wish I believed
my God would understand
—my arm linked
into yours made him
unnecessary.
The cornices
of these high balconies
are full of distress.
Below
nuns anoint themselves
in holy water,
their faces quiet
with denial.
Like the angels
who have no sweat,
their bodies

always heavenward,
their touch
is not intimate.
Even if I light
these candles,
the black Easter wax,
the mourning candles
of Good Friday,
even if I cross myself regularly,
I am, love,
without God, and you
remain absent.

The Street of the Aphrodite Hotel

Where is the pity
in the empty streets we traveled
without pity?

Despair is there
in the empty streets, but
where is the pity?

Though pain has laid bare
the whole of ourselves, we loved
without pity

every step down that street, in plaintive
belief, in the stave we repeat,
Where is the pity

we sought in the hope of repair?
In abandon and nerve we lived the affair
without pity.

Tell me our brave state was not
some fool fate, answer me . . .
without pity.

Opened

In a medieval city stuccoed with baroque porticoes,
hidden in courtyards mapped in vines,
he says 'like suicide' and I slowly nod,
his focus on me. Gradually
I understand the accumulated
slivered knife-nicks at the vulnerable flesh,
the final cut, 'a free-fall' I say
as if it were a fiction, one I have fallen in love with,
a rapture of revenge: 'I cut' I repeat and scissor my fingers
to enact the gesture as he nods, performing
the necessity of this assurance. He says the one who leaves
is the strong one. I am silent. He repeats the certainty—
and the word surfaces again, *suicide*. I think
instead of or *like* as crucial as
the violence of the violet colors in the park,
the happiness of the days here, and the peculiar emptiness
of this café. I am nodding *yes*
as the true picture of this forms itself: felled body,
person, hope severed—amputated.
He describes a vampirish taking, a girlfriend's
random changes, distant when he was soft, needy
when he was distant; we are, suddenly, two, the two of us
in this place where the city's stone feels material
where we are burying our pasts in excavated spaces.

Brides

Elina describes the DVD she watched late last night: after 7 years
this couple finally manage to be together & marry,

there's a scene where the bride's making breakfast for the two of them,
spills milk when her man gets up to help her out and they make love,

she goes back to getting the coffee to boil when he goes into the shower
but she's done something, the milk, the boiler, something short circuits

and she's electrocuted, her husband comes screaming out of the shower,
Elina's telling me she was screaming too when her son, a 17 year old,

thought something was really wrong only to find her crying in front of the TV
like me 3 nights ago watching *Nifes* with my 15 year old daughter

who brought the movie home, the story of mail-order brides in 1920s Greece,
a country of poverty, raw hills, islands barely freed of Turks when

a young woman, Niki, agrees to be given to a man she has never seen
to save the family. There's the long boat ride to America with another 650 mail-

order brides from Russia and other Greek islands, a last shot of life as Niki
the independent seamstress she yearns to be, all the brides' slim bodies like lilies,

their expressions fragile, their hair wound and bound like women walking
to a sacrifice. Everyone's below deck where they're sailing to futures they

hardly imagine, the islands and homes of childhood now 'a place my children
will never know' a girl from Limnos says as I'm weeping on the couch,

my daughter's arm around me as I keep repeating *no one gets what they want.*
The photographer, an Irish-American by the name of Norman, is in love

with Niki, enraptured with her nicked fingertips, her broken English while she,
the stern island girl, tells him in tears and passion that she cannot be

with him, that she must give herself to Prodromos, the man she is promised to,
to save the seven sisters left behind, to afford the colored pencils

she will send back to her youngest sister Norman says 'you must miss' when
Niki answers 'I don't miss her, I love her.' And the movie ends with Niki's

tightly wound hair cut into an American bob, her figure hugged by an expensive
red dress as she reads the letter Norman managed to stash into a box of

photographs *I don't want you to never have received a love letter,*
I want you to know you are the being I will miss all my life

Glass

Let's say she has no fairy godmother.
Let's say one of her stepsisters
really does manage to force her foot
into the glass slipper and triumphant marries
the bewildered prince.
Cinderella is left to gather the frayed moments,
clothing too worn for even the needy.
And I walk away from the fairytale
of ever-waiting love rewarded with the prince
or any story of princesses who know love
is everlasting. In my arms
you were unable to say my arms,
my eyes, the lips you kissed
brought you to my arms, my eyes, the lips
you kissed and kissed, so the lost
slipper left by any Cinderella
so drunk on happiness she slips in her step
from the dance, fits any stepsister
who insists its hers, and pushes hard enough.

Ritual

I throw out useless potatoes, soggy
onions in thinned skins, like grief
smelling of rot. I think of my daughter
in the shower, friends caught in narrow lives
—nothing spectacular, the floorboard sounds,
my neighbor's movements, men who've left scents
in my dreams, that one lost face, this
pavement in rain, nothing spectacular, this
dumping of the trash, its full thud, I do it
without much thought. Strange
how I see my daughter's wet hair, her body,
a cleansed altar.

The Border

Ruska is preparing for the dawn trip
to Bulgaria, years since she saw
her two sons Ivan and Evgenio,
but they are still small and when asked
what they want for Christmas
they say 'mother.'
What Ruska fears is not
the village gossip, that she has lived
these years in Greece with another man,
or the unemployment she is sure
to find on her return, the shortness
of food and freedom.
What she fears is the border.
The men at the station stop
will force them off the bus in the black
winter chill, decide the hours,
even days, of their waiting
in some infinite space of doom.
They will make fun of the cargo,
spit slow laughter
at the luggage of life,
so dispensable—the packets, bags,
nudged and kicked, the contents
of an impossible life: Ruska
who left her sons at 22, penniless.
In Greece it was possible to hope
to return after having
gathered the money
to make a life. At this border
Ruska fears the soldiers will rip
through the bags, even her body,
toys will spill across the hardened ground,
tiny gold crosses will show

through torn linings, clothes
will be shredded as her frozen hands
will gesture dumbly.
Crossing over into homeland
would have meant making it back
through so much pain.

Zoi Se Mas

Stavros hugs me, holds my hand as we
pass names along the marble slabs,
grave dates, some with pictures.
'That's Lakis, there,' he tells his wife Maria.
'It's a shame,' she mumbles. We trudge
in a crowd of black clad to the opened ditch.
Raw earth in piles, the shovels scraping soil
into the torn hole where Vyron's casket has been lowered.
Stavros nods, says '67 years,' and starts to cry,
his tall body shaken in the goodbye.
He throws a clump of earth over the buried man,
his friend of 67 years whose books of law
lined all his walls, who counted
400 places *fos*, Greek for light, surfaced
in Sikleanos' poetry. Vyron never flew
in a plane, or moved from the neighborhood.
Friends and family are gathered,
his wife Poppie's tears drench her face.
Poppie's sister smiles at my name,
'your father's old bills and tax receipts
still come to our house.' My father is far away
so I am here instead. My mother on the phone
long-distance keeps her emotion checked.
'Your father is so upset, why is everyone disappearing
so quickly?' Stavros and Vyron and my father
lived on the same street, until my father flew
so far the distance devoured him.
I sit with Stavros and Maria. She tells me
it was Vyron's barking dog that
introduced them, 'three doors down from me,
that's where he lived.' Maria's nails are freshly red.
She is slowly losing her mind to Alzheimer's
but understands the day, says, 'We are in line now.

Life is for the young.' Stavros is shaking hands
with a judge who says, 'Still here?'
'For a little while,' Stavros smiles and sips
the cognac we drink to Vyron's memory: '*Zoi
se mas,*' we say and I think of the piles of books
in Vyron's apartment, piles and piles of them, and then
the dirt, and the shovels, and his face as he would sit,
pensive, listening.

Stassi Ecclesia

1

The bus is large
going up a narrow
village street, and so far
all the stops
have been wrong.
A man offers
night flowers, soft
white crosses bloom
in his voice,
the bus doors
open
and shut
quickly, his voice
is crushed
petals.
Then I meet someone
who cooks
with homemade spices,
the nails of his fingers,
tiny and short
like our meals,
like our increasingly
shortened conversations.
I enjoy
the champagne light,
count orchards
through the window,
smell boundless
scents of earth

2

I don't recognize
the faces I
pay attention to, the ones
I hardly see,
and when the bus lurches to a halt,
my body, thrown
into a stranger's arms, falls,
and he with me. There are no guarantees
of the company,
the people who get off, or
stay on. Paul was planning
to finish the novel
he had been writing
for years. We talked a lot
between classes. He urged me
to look for work
elsewhere, since the school's
financial trouble
meant we might be
without jobs.
'I'm done' he smiled,
about to retire at 61
readying to ease himself
into a slower pace.
'For some reason' he said,
'I feel optimistic
about things.' It was July,
we were having coffee
in the sun. In September
Paul was buried.
We scattered *koliva*
40 days after

his death, the barley
and wheat grains, raisins
and pomegranate seeds eaten
in his memory,
thrown to birds

3
In the dream the bus
keeps mistaking the stop.
In the dream
I take down
mugs from a kitchen shelf
and find unwashed
traces of thirst
inside the porcelain
bottoms, smudge
marks I can't wash off.
I recognize
a turn, cliff banks,
then darkness,
a hill I am climbing barefoot
amid shards glinting
in thin light,
the city is distant
scattered glass,
massive candles spill
yellow over
the top of a hill,
past the beautiful stone
houses in an empty space,
up steps
to what I believe is
salvation.

Epitaph

He became a lip of land
overcome by waves
and battle, and then the settling of time—
silt and dust on the sun's tongue.
So when I hear he wants to be in touch
I imagine a voice belonging
to glyphs now unfamiliar
and say 'no' and mean the scrolls of hymns
buried with the Pharaoh's things
did not survive. The songs quickly shredded
on pages that were not papyrus, and he
remains incomplete history.

I Could Want

his hand, the smile
that eludes me. I could want
a childhood that never happened.
I nudge the cat asleep at my feet,
her shape cushioned. I am envious of cushions,
expectant mothers, the curve that protects,
his clutching of my entire back
in love. I could want a future of love.
I could want to protect my daughter
with the fierce cushionings I did not have. I could
go about feeding live souls, the cat, the parrot.
I could manage the half expectation
of his wants without wanting more, I could want
that he want more, and know he cannot
manage more. She has an expression in her eyes,
her gaze elsewhere, wanting. I could tell her
of my failed desires, I could assure her
of the effort that ropes in boats
when open sea scatters them. I could want
to never stop reaching toward her,
her own boat unanchored beyond what I can
cushion or reach. There's so much I want
to tell her. I could want what I don't have to give,
give what I don't have.

Belated

Death again, but not of the spoiled lemons, blackened
in a late frost, ruined at their moment of ripeness,

nor of badly pruned branches, cut callously
with blunt shears, the stringy sinews still green.

The life might have been saved had they known
the danger, the waters sapphire in gorgeous lagoons,

deep, the currents invisible, had they known
the swimmer better, to warn him of the nets and

winds, that weather is fickle and the islanders
too wedded to their own survival to know how

to warn the innocent man of things they take for granted.

Random Heaven

I want to say 'beauty' not 'flowers' has overrun
this place and hugs what blooms in these
fields of straggling green. Not the obvious lavender pretties,
the exhibitionists, the ones I want to cut at the root—
no, 'beauty' is this despite-itself-happiness you feel,
un-metaphorical—white puckered, the lovely
grape hyacinth perfection
in the impossible glare of the day.
What I think I'm trying to say is
what I saw this morning was close to glory.

After the path through garbage where the chamomile grows
and poppies wave in the occasional breeze where weeds
braid their leaves through the barely possible grass, and
the sun-blessed reluctant daisies keep nodding, I kept thinking
I wish I had the soul of the soil to nourish this
planted-nowhere-in-particular-heaven
where patches of loveliness might save the rotting tire
and Styrofoam scraps from their soulless demise, where
the filthy, rain-drenched jeans wedged beneath
the fallen trunk, might be resurrected,
cleaned and ironed and given to a needy refugee.

Or like the story of the boy who ate at Baskin-Robbins
until he was over 300 pounds and no woman would go near him,
let alone kiss and hug his large, hurt self
until he decided he would manage to believe in something
he could not yet see or feel and lost the weight, and found the woman,
I would bless the acrid scents rising from the peat
of mixed debris, and hope the squashed stems flower.

But how to save those tiny virgin somethings, the dots of white
scattered through these chunks of rusting metal parts?
The black-eyed ruby sprigs keep bending coyly in their nonchalance.
I see my aging parents in the burdened olive branch,
my sullen father who refused the sun's bouquets. My mother
who twists her wedding band and prays, mulls over
how a steel mill worker's daughter married a Greek
who hardly spoke English, how the dead he'd seen in war
forever marked his love, yet she like mint kept seeking out the sun
in the heat that seeds this rooted splurge of color.

From One Minute to the Next

The girls are weeping in my daughter's room, the boys
walk quietly to where the wheels spun from the ground, run their hands along
the wall as if their touch could bring him back. They feel the sun's drenched
heat. They feel their grief and speak of him, always

on his BMX, his curly hair, his almond eyes. I remember
the skating rink events, his pretty mother tugging at his hand,
him pulling back for another round on the ice and she speaking hurriedly
that they must go, smiling when I said he must be a handful.

That was when we got together for the birthday party rounds,
when our kids were really young, and we, the parents, drank coffees
at park cafés, ate popcorn and gossiped to pass the time until
from one minute to the next, or so it seemed, our kids didn't want us around

and the curly brown-haired boy went to another school, told, this time
without humor, that he was a handful because he couldn't sit still, because he
was the kind of boy who drove the teachers crazy because he couldn't sit still,
because he wanted to be outside playing volleyball or on his skateboard,

wanted to go everywhere on his bicycle like his closest buddy, a boy
who kept him company on his own BMX weaving through the thoroughfares,
jumping sidewalks to go faster, finding short cuts, the way the kids
remembered the two buddies on their bikes, in their own world, they said,

when one of the boys spoke of how the beautiful boy tried to make a campfire
on a balcony when they were in the seventh grade, how they'd take the
supermarket shopping carts, wheeling themselves and their bags to the nearby
hamburger place. Then from one minute to the next,

or so it seemed, the beautiful boy was sixteen, and his buddy, seventeen,
who drove a car that took them further than anywhere they could go
on their bikes, drove to the shore, up mountain roads, and now that they were
almost men, the girls started to talk of how the beautiful boy

was going to be the hottest of them all, was going to be the hottest of them all,
the beautiful boy they realized how much they loved when his buddy
drove off the road and from one minute to the next the beautiful boy's head
was crushed in blood, his body without a pulse, and his buddy

began to run as fast as his legs could take him into the flow of cars and trucks,
the lunatic boy trying to die with his friend. Instead cars stopped and he
was taken crazed to a hospital, and the beautiful boy, the beautiful, curly
brown-haired boy who couldn't sit still was laid out in his coffin

and his pretty mother, now older but still pretty lay draped over the still wood
that held her beautiful son, and my daughter and her classmates
stood dressed in their best as if for a celebration when his father asked
if they would like to take their friend to his grave, carry his coffin

on their shoulders, saying he would have liked that, to be circled a last time
by those who loved him and filled his casket with what he loved most,
tangerines, energy chocolate bars and his dismantled bicycle.

Before the Ship Arrives

Night and the wait is long.
A woman laughs into her drink.
A rough man wishes someone good sleep.
I notice a cross, the church unlit,
and right above, or next to it,
a half moon fastened to the black.
And in the parked car next to mine, waiting
for the ship to take us home, is someone
sleeping, a bird cage on its side,
the parrot inside, a woman with her leg
stretched over the dashboard, and the man
I wish to hear from is out of reach.
Savage, the clarity of this hour.

Holy Agony

"The names we give very often fail to make Him there"
—Rhina P. Espaillat speaking on "Poetry and Religion"

Balkan Voices

Jofka
Other people's lives have an intimate smell.
The woman I work for has rows of
clothes, so many colors hang in her closet.
I wear my black jersey skirt, my jean shirt.
Aubergine she said. *Aubergine* is what I remember
the night I stay to babysit the child.
For these hours I own the quiet.
The night lamp turns the color brown wine,
the color I put against my skin. *Aubergine.*
I always put the underwear back in the drawer.

Tamara
The sheets begin to smell of my tears.
The old lady tells her daughter
she cannot sleep at night
because of my tears. She is very old,
at night she makes the throaty sounds of the dying.
I think her smell is always on me.
I go out to the tiny balcony
to breathe, but the smell clings.
There is none of this in my letters to Katia.
I write as I spoke in the war.
Without food or hope I spoke of food and hope.
They must manage without me.
It's like I have died, but I speak anyway—
The money is sewn into the pillowslip.
Buy shoes. Send your uncle the pills . . . courage,

remember we have survived war.
My leaving Tibilisi was easy
then worse than war; I could not touch
my daughters' faces.

Natalia
The wind blows red
island dust, dirt, my face clogs
with the red in my pores. Red water
comes off my skin.
For months even the towel comes away
red.
We had good jobs in Bulgaria.
Then everything closed,
we had to find work
in fields where dirt
flies in your face like a blown shirt.

Tamara
The color of the sky when I left Georgia,
the color of war, the color of mornings
I had to think how we would eat, the color
of vegetables in oil, vegetables in salt,
wilted vegetables, the color floods me.
I would say 'eat,' I would say
'I'm not hungry.' Katia would say
'no mama, you eat. You work.'
'I'm too tired,' I would say and think
they are growing, they need the food, I would even
laugh. I'm always telling lies to feed them.

Vania
It is a deep, bone deep loneliness
as if light alone

clothes me. I admire the ochre
shaping what my body is.
The walls shaped in this
light hear me as I pass them to work,
every day an impossibility
I enter, ordered to by God
who will not return me
to Bulgaria. He will
have me travel this land that doesn't
belong to me. I cannot
turn back, like Lot's wife
I will disappear if I turn.

Tamara
They do not know this: how I clean
another person's house
like it is my own. I was raised to live
in my home. What could be wrong
in the old woman's world?
She worries about her floors, the dust.
I say 'Tamara, you have this dust
in Georgia. You are cleaning your home in Georgia.'
In my dreams
my house is coated in Georgian dirt
and smells of rain.

Vania
This morning I didn't want to wake from my dream.
I was sleeping with my arms around my son.
I could smell his hair, ash-trees.
I could smell his skin, vanilla and bitter lemon.
I could touch his arms, long tender lengths.
I could warm his skin, the coolness behind the knees.

Jofka
I am a refugee in open space.
This is who I am now, a color
like the poppies in spring.
Lilacs and wild daisies
climb the embankments. One day
the line is somewhere on a far mountain,
the next it is drawn across
another mountain. The flowers grow wild everywhere.
We travel the lines,
gather clothes, our blankets,
red like the poppies, yellow like chaff.
I sew dark yellow lines
around the flowers.
They've bombed a factory
next to an orphanage
in Kosovo, now it will run its chemicals
across the lines. People are so stupid. There will only be
one color in the end,
a single dull rust.
Not even red, after the flames and blood
this color will be
a smell that crosses lines.

Tamara
I am so many pieces
anyway, it doesn't matter anymore.
What's one more lost tooth,
one more meal of potatoes
and days-old bread.
I am heavy with days-old bread and potatoes,
starve with them.
When I touch

my girls I'm full, I'm Tamara.
Now I'm losing
the last parts of Tamara.

Vania
No more blood, I tell her,
no more red. She cannot understand.
It's over, I say. The red has stopped.
She says she knows,
because I'm from Sofia.
She says communism is finished.
It's not communism I tell her.
What? she says.
My blood is over.
Your blood?
Yes, I say, I'm 38.
I cannot have babies anymore.

Tamara
In all my dreams Katia is speaking
Mother you have been everything we know the world by . . .
Ina is practical. She writes of how many
blankets to send, she writes of my brother's leg.
I must send bandages, medicine, even
cotton with money for the doctor.

Jofka
The TV, the small vacuum cleaner,
the dollars Ivan managed to find, all our
drachmas, exchanged for dollars,
stolen. He stood in the kitchen with a smile,
a knife in his hand, telling us to leave.
The educated schoolteacher,

the schoolteacher criminal. No,
just the criminal.
If he was a schoolteacher in Albania,
he's a criminal now. He laughed,
his wife laughed. Ivan, my husband, tried to talk.
He told him he didn't want a fight.
The criminal laughed again, played with the knife,
leaned against the kitchen counter,
told us he was tired of living with us.
Ivan said we would pack our things.
The criminal said everything stays
with the house, Ivan tried
to talk to him. He just laughed again.
Then I started laughing
loudly. I laughed and laughed and laughed.
Tears were in my eyes and my stomach
ached. I didn't stop. The last thing I remember is
Ivan sitting me down on a bench
where people were passing, staring.
I was still laughing.
Ivan called Thanassi, the man
he works for in the car repair shop.
Ivan, pale in the street light,
pale when he sat down next to me, said
Thanassi would help me
go back to Albania.

Natalia
The result is the same, even if
she was polite. She asked me to leave.
I'm not a beggar.
I will find work. I found fields
ripe in olives, red dirt.
I didn't realize

I banged the door as I let it
swing into a curse. Words.
I went to a church to calm the words,
light a candle.
A child lay in a basket,
the priest's sleeve
brushed against its cheek.
Children cradled candied boxes.
The baby cried,
the poor thing
has no idea
incense smells, candle smells,
altar flowers
in vases,
will not soften
the shock. Naked,
baptized or not, it will learn
a name.
Christian, Greek
or Russian,
Muslim or Jewish, everyone fights
for a name they believe holy.
I shouldn't have come
to church, shouldn't have
banged the door.
My name is Natalia, it means
nothing on this earth,
the field will bury it like all
the fallen olives.

Tamara
Katia's letter says my brother died,
even with the money
I sent for the leg operation. It's the first time

I didn't cry after a letter from Katia.
I will go back to Georgia now,
to my daughters' full embrace,
the fertile land, the rusted spades,
the blue plum trees, back
to tomatoes and corn and potatoes,
to pickled vegetables in jars,
to milk from the old goat, back
to the exposed brick walls of the apartment,
to toilet paper so thick it scratches my skin, back
to boarded up porches, ripped plaster
ceilings, to the dimness of 30-watt light, back
to braids of red pepper, to laundry
on balcony railings hanging above gardens,
many colored and everywhere
strung across window frames.

Places & Names

Numbers in War—*Kolokithia*, a village in northern Greece. During WWII the guerrilla fighters won a battle there and took over the village from Nazi Germans. Hitler's edict was that for every German killed 100 Greeks must be executed. If they didn't have prisoners they picked civilians. For a wounded German, the ratio was 50 to 1.

"Are You Listening?"—The Mekong River runs from Tibet though China, Laos, Thailand, and Cambodia and into the South-China Sea, considered one of the 10 longest rivers in the world. Also referred to as 'the haunted river' because of its witness to war, particularly the Vietnam War (1965-1973), known too as the Second Indochina War.

Setting Out—A title and poem in conversation with W. B. Yeats' "Sailing to Byzantium" and C. P. Cavafy's "The City".

Looks & Wants—italicized words in the first paragraph spoken by Condoleezza Rice in a TV interview on the Iraq intervention.

Critical Maps—Omar Khayyam, a Sufi poet (c.1047- c.1122), wrote "The Rubaiyat" translated by Edward Fitzgerald in 1859.

Yassir—Pontian for one who is downtrodden; *kotsari*, a heel dance and *kementze*, the Pontian lyre. "A language almost gone" refers to Pontic Greek or Rüm once spoken in northern mountain villages along the coast of the Black Sea; Kemal Atatürk's campaign to eliminate the Christian minorities (Armenians, Assyrians and Pontians) between 1915 and 1923 destroyed the communities that spoke this language. Italics from *Not Even My Name* by Thea Halo. The poem was written for Jordan Karatzas.

Letters Home—Italicized phrases from Margaret Fuller's letters in *The Letters of Margaret Fuller*, Vol. V: 1848-49. Edited by Robert N. Hudspeth.

The Uneasy Equation of Space and Form—"Milosz' more spacious form" refers to Czeslaw Milosz' "Ars Poetica?" in which he writes: "I have always aspired to a more spacious form/ that would be free from the claims of poetry or prose/and would let us understand each other without exposing/ the author or reader to sublime agonies.//" From *Bells In Winter*.

Xeni, Xenos, Xenitia—*Xeni*: foreigner (female); *Xenos*: foreigner (male); *Xenitia*, one forced to live in foreign lands or away from home, generally used to describe the state of Greek migrants. *Xenitia* (from *xenia*, hospitality) could be read as that of being a guest abroad. This poem is for Katerina Anghelaki-Rooke.

Neos Kosmos—'New world' in Greek, also a neighborhood off the main thoroughfare of Vouliagmenis St. in Athens.

Her Sexy Hunger—*Yiayia*, Greek for grandmother.

Fall Grapes— *Mustos* Greek for 'must', the expressed juice of grapes before and during fermentation.

The Benediction—*Koliva*, a mix of boiled wheat, raisins, pomegranate seeds, candied almonds and other nuts offered as tribute to the passing of the soul; traditionally prepared by the family of the departed at Greek funerals as a gesture toward nourishing the living with the memory of the departed.

The Street of the Aphrodite Hotel—Refers to Apollonos Street in Plaka. The Aphrodite Hotel has been renamed Hotel Hermes.

Brides—The poem's title is translated from the Greek *Nifes*, a 2004 movie by Pandelis Voulgaris.

Zoi Se Mas—'Life to us' (in Greek), as in 'Life be with us' a wish expressed at Greek funerals.

Belated—For Panayiotis (Paul) Angelides, 1942- 2004.

From One Minute to the Next—For Aristidi (Ari) Komborozou, 1990-2006.

Balkan Voices - After the fall of the Eastern bloc there was a steady influx into Greece of Bulgarians, Albanians, Russians, and other nationals from and into the Balkans looking for work and repatriation.

Biographical Note

Adrianne Kalfopoulou is the author of *Wild Greens*, a poetry collection from Red Hen Press, and a prose memoir, *Broken Greek*. She has also published two chapbooks, *FIG* and *CUMULUS*. *Passion Maps* is her second collection of poems. She has taught workshops at the University of Edinburgh's international summer program as well as workshops in Greece and is currently an assistant professor at Hellenic American University in Athens where she developed the general education program and teaches literature.